FIGMENT

The Barnard Women Poets Prize

EDITED BY SASKIA HAMILTON

Also by Rebecca Wolff

Manderley

figment

Rebecca Wolff

W. W. Norton & Company
New York • London

For information about permission to reproduce selections from this book,
write to Permissions, W. W. Norton & Company, Inc., 500 Fifth Avenue,
New York, NY 10110

Manufacturing by Courier Westford
Book design by Julia Druskin

Library of Congress Cataloging-in-Publication Data

Wolff, Rebecca, 1967–
Figment / Rebecca Wolff.—1st ed.
p. cm.
ISBN 0-393-05918-9 (hardcover)
I. Title.
PS3623.O56F54 2004
811'.6—dc22

2003016737

W. W. Norton & Company, Inc., 500 Fifth Avenue, New York, N.Y. 10110
www.wwnorton.com

W. W. Norton & Company Ltd., Castle House, 75/76 Wells Street, London
W1T 3QT

1 2 3 4 5 6 7 8 9 0

For Ira

Here is where a quote from a song would have gone, but for the lack of permission. The song is "Dig a Pony," off the album *Let It Be*, and in this song John Lennon declares, with many variations, that it is possible for one to "indicate" anything or everything one "sees." This is one of my favorite songs.

"Dig a Pony" was largely made up in the studio and the words make very little sense. At one point it was called "Con A Lowry" (possibly a reference to a make of organ used in the studio) but John changed it to "Dig A Pony" "because 'I con a Lowry' didn't sing well . . . It's got to be d's and p's, you know."

—www.geocities.com/SunsetStrip/Palms/6797/songs/digapony.html

Contents

Acknowledgments

My thanks to the editors of the following journals, print and online, in which some of these poems first appeared:

The Ampersand, Boston Review, Bridge, canwehaveourball-back?, The Canary, The Colorado Review, CrossCultural Poetics, Crowd, GutCult, nowculture.com, NC2, Papertiger (Australia), Paris Review, Post Road, Salt Hill, The Southeast Review, The Transcendental Friend, Washington Square.

"Autobiographia Copularia" was printed first in *The Portable Boog Reader*, Kirschenbaum, David A., ed., New York, Boog Literature, 2000.

That Impulse

Life of Sorts

Stopping under the speaking tree

tracing the lines of my own face
with well lubricated fingertips

I am not now
nor ever have I been

free with myself,
and you know why that is.

If I could only learn to make the perfect skirt
I would never work again.

My own line. "To what do you attribute
your success?" Talent *and* genius.

A talent for genius: Crows paired up in the black tree
lift off metonymically,

two feathers ride an invincible,
blooded draft. My life

as an activist
begins.

A good idea, but not well executed

In the mirror catching glimpses
of a vale of other aspects—
always taught, when yet a child
that people were basically good. By example,
I was taught. Mother smiling and communing
on the street with bums and hustlers,
sometimes frenching the janitor. By inference
I concluded I was also,
basically, good. *Now the frothing,*
now declaiming, now the mutilation and the frottage.
The defrocking. When we come as visitors
we make gifts of fruit and thrush.
Part of the essential
process of maturation you must acknowledge
faulty design, craftsmanship, constitution.
A first draft: "Why the very idea,
to suddenly lose consciousness!"

A marriage
is not made for exploration; nylon
is not made to let the air through
to your skin. Why the very *idea*
of that shy smile is convertible,

something about gorgeous, contour
of reflected movement, the corpse a
head shaking "no" on the table

padded the last smile essentially
gorgeous as the essentialist statement. This chair
has no footholds it is designed for ejection. I am
to be cut open for the first time tomorrow. What slips out
in the future to be sent to the lab
to addict my arm.

Unexpected movement and a black spot
in the corner of my eye, reflected out. Until
that moment I had a very painful sense
of not belonging to this world, but then
a sweet breath flew from the mouth of the Northeast,
the last thing you want to be familiar with,
flush of unlove. Oh Mama

your baby in the future

Autobiographia Copularia

after Frank O'Hara
as per Marjorie Welish

I fell ill
and then when I wasn't ill anymore

like all children
I missed my illness. It had kept me

from so much.
Like all children, I had never really wanted

to go outside—
fairs, rides, clowns, bundling, clones, the

spent, the sweat.
Expend in stealth, keep your shirt on, feed

without the fervor.
There is a place for autobiography:

in the home.
Meeting other people and fucking them never

entered my mind.

Eminent Victorians

Half the day is dead already—
a lady with a baby in the shady graveyard
promenade not quite the idea
but the first idea to be impressed
so firmly—Grace to be born

in the
bisected quadrangle
stones propped insensible
but all in relation
to the babe.

Babe what suckles
babe what grows comfortable with thieves in a fertile
bed of unsaid
slice of eponymous
grafted to the reef

Hold my hand
in the undergrowth
waist high at your leisure cheerful
child of melancholy and displeasure.
Soft in the lap you grow

hard at the breast—Oh
under- and aboveground we go
to relieve us. Camphor

and cambric by the hand not by halves,
one turn more

will take us back to where we rest.
Baby is not baby when she
wears her oblong
freshet
I will take her home to rest.

Obsolete Coin

In diverse groups
and agitated form
some feeling comes

through opened shade
diskette stove away
nostalgic abalone

I tried so hard
then put a stop
but Nothing paid attention

to the quality of light.
Closed form: An agitated
feeling comes

its classical depth
a time machine, gadget
cheating for fame's

elegiacal wampum.
I paid to come: Frost,
mist, smoke, valley, ridge, and vaporous

the shadowy urge,
the call I've put in
for some, remember, munificence.

I can remember heaving that way.
The breath of the Creator: deep in the trough, cycling
through irreversibility.

A Longer Leash

The body closest to me
too careful to be dead
took cues I could only dream of

tripping through the gate

finger, a disembodied word
ribs cracking from the inside
no treasury of cyclamen—

another flower name distasted.

While it is luxurious sitting
down to write it is privation
to be without the proper

tools: flower name
purported misconstrued, flower
name contracted to the insides

and back to privilege: growing
up not amongst vocabularies
but into a gardeners'

chapter. Flags of detail,
eros charter. Fountain of flower-lover
come to naught, direct-mail

narcissus, paperwhite in gutter
home's eventual return to me. Sparrow
come to sip from the shallow pool of water

poured
of meaning to be potent, to be married,
to correct congenital defects.

Tripping over the gate
brush the dust off African
violet

and arrive at tons of petals

come to recognize their features: particular
obsessions, f'rinstance, pruned
like fruit trees. The syntax

hasn't cleared up yet, I see.
And take your cue not from the world
[insert list of names of flowers,

botanical, vernacular].
Irony is mimicry.
Visitors are consumers.

4:30 Lakeshore Limited Was in the Past

repeatedly, being strong
long ago
we started to move

to stifle that impulse
next to take care of:
full sacs
of glands inside the sack
the poetry you're writing

is not exactly exciting
declension of rattlesnake.

Instruction in passion—no bundling
no cheap diorama
batteries
potato chips
many other items
full weight of majority

the view is to the left
straggler, disallowed
and after a while
my neck starts in on hurting.
Calamity had a special

reason: Come inside my warm

and friendly life, the other
one I haven't shown
you with meditations in it
on the position of loved ones.
On the bed, usually, on the couch

expectantly. I derive
how to expect
from your mountain
of goodness.

It's been so long
since I was weak and wrote
to tell you so.
And in that time

da dum da dum
you never need to know.
Wanderlust consecrated,

a diamond-dragon
in registers of "What is fierce?
What is holy."
Look at the shining river
uncovered
by cloud, by sky, nonvegetable
education. Could I grow to be

a train conductor?
Harmonious
in little ways, not the ways
I have been shown
automatically, my neighbor
humming like a tuning fork
rectitudinally

program of grace
I've got it all over her
eyelids, like hoods they are
but she lifts them.
It worked out
in the end,
the sky achieving height above
the window.

Imagine that I drink a can of beer
every day at four o'clock
and watch the sun get a little
low. That's the lyric.

I know how I get.
That impulse.

I walk the property line

Yonder fragile, yonder day
de-pilled and set inside endemic construct. Dark shade
on the patch of grass where

I'm who I always wanted to be. Want
consolidated
in the sun-baked center stays put.

You want to sit on grass but not get lost in it—Meanwhile

I inherit some kind of
drag un-conception, this smallness
of indication; a funnel finds me: Exorcism.
The sun moves around me, captivated
as a race horse would be
by the magic test of sentences.

. . .

Find me again in a situation: flash-frozen
arena. The largest clearing in my town
is a ball-field, ringed around
by native pines and scrub.

I wish I never made you, savage semblance. You play unbidden, you
point always in the same direction and the sun
moves around you in torpor. It's

unbecoming, this display
of crushing naiveté, but so full of feeling
am I, I am flushed in the
diurnal/draconian fashion of a sundial. Nations

tell their time this way.

. . .

A formal invitation,
the freedom to write

diminishing return.

Really I mean it

I'm so sick of cabal:
besleeved at the séance—

Century's inclusion.

. . .

Swing around in the overcast.
You've sauntered to the edge to see

what's living in a thicket, what's pushed
to flaw's perimeter, but start running

fast away when you spy
movement. The knapsack makes its breathing noise,

all ingredients in broad daylight:
toadstool, wrapper, gaily colored debris from innocents

blowing up things.
Firestorm of open sky framed like this,
Saturated, streaked. It's wholly made of one thing.
Give it back its termination.

Dark shade on the patch of grass where

I leave nothing behind when I leave there.

Public Space: Suite

I was woefully under-briefed
for an important tele-
conference. But my legs

are commercially long—
they carried me across town
like a taxi to

Assisted Suicide: a Café Bistro.
Convention of literary fiction.
Proven insufficient
                              (not enough)
in, literally, a dialect
                              (vernacular)
to just keep passing the pedestrians
without harming them. The arm lashes out
faster than connotation.

On the sidewalk all is business-
minded. Black looks
shooting from depressions. I am white
so set it all to music.
One small boy cries
righteously at the pace
his mother sets to trot
him down the inclement path. A fine
rain sprays vexation on his blubbering

puss; without the ordering
principle everything
is boring. *Note that this*
diagram has been distorted primarily
to portray the service clearly.

. . .

This is a real part of my life:
getting a job. Pure sadness.
When you know the right people,
or a few who care enough
to take the time
to send the very best
they send you over onto the next
in line. They return your calls. And bring you
down to the transfer office,
looking a lot like a subway station.

Pressed the flesh all day in the service.
"Excuse me can you please stop touching me?"
at all the points at which you are touching me,
however incidentally . . . *wrist knee tristesse conjecture tyranny.*
A banquette for one
has masterminded. One has outlasted
one's own irrelevance
the disorganized

disorgan

I am not sure we come
underground for entertainment.

. . .

And now I finally accept
that a person is the sum of their accomplishments
as rendered in *skills*. I still can't
ski. I can't be bothered
with packaging. My agent is marketing
me to a client
for me. Another

Probe. Sex-machine
in corporate drab. Promise
of derangement and eviction, self-inflicted,
it's the crisis of our age.
Public space
commission.
A buzzword. "She is extremely *project-oriented*.
She loves the word 'project' and the word
that means doing projects well . . . you know . . .
performance."

I'm always working
I'm always thinking

how it's better than plowing furrows
it's better than whipping horses
it sure beats digging ditches

. . .

Everyone's always insisting
that desire is not rational.
Up front with the halt and the lame
on the Lexington Avenue line
I am at eye level. Oh please
come and love me
                    (knowing you are)
the morning in devolution
                    (higher form)

"But how will you get home, so late
so late?"
"Oh," blithely,
"I'll travel underground,
with lively lightness
                    (and no fear)
and of what I am unconscious."
Engaged in higher wisdom
invested in purer motive
when the subway has come
to seem a natural resting place

I am one step closer
to the grand disinvestiture. With stars
dropping like flies
all around us

why are you so homeless?
I don't understand why you're so homeless.

The Sustained Project

1. BEASTLY MATRONLY

The season was open and it called to me—
an informality
Dozens of wooden soldiers
More than the usual army
None of the usual goose-stepping here though

It all happens so fast—
ovulation, creation, cremation. I certainly don't believe
any of these historical figures ever
existed, said these words or
constructed those tremendous
arches

But I could murder you
with this toothpick if I wanted;
retinally inscribe
my extremity (lot in life)

Schedule as attachment
liking that informality
all told
blood-doping
manumission
the things I see when I open my eyes, unadvised

"Never look upon a stranger
for more than a minute.
As in a dream, he becomes your reality
and, taking your hand, makes

a menace of himself." Potent,
ambitious, a driving force

in the business of conclusion,
a young one with a following already
behind him. In my breast

together with the rest.

2. CHANGING ITS CHARACTER

I look stronger than I am
Given to us to evolve out of what now?
Wearing a flowered dress
on a hot day—what is that anymore?
I do not wish to leave my home
—not out of fear
but because it is more beautiful

the trees have gathered there

good—the rain will hold the dust down

A new subject?
quantifiable, not like my fragrance.

With an entomologist's curiosity

I tell you phone
              phone
the only matter is light

Spatially, in the physical plane,
then you fan out and find their ways.

3. Inquire Within

Put a cap on it
Any opportunity for rest
Now you have reached the limits
of my intelligence.

Not properly described as a scheme
more a reason
to be young, white, and serial.
If your sign said "I'm lonely"
we would sit down beside you
on the sidewalk.

Sit outside,
all your dressing, transparent.
"And what if she can't speak? Or hear
or see"—what if she is a character in a movie
Beating a retreat
from the public self
under the road (troll)

4. STOMA

Out of sight out of mind
Terrestrial basis
Memento of
Childhood's prognosis:
Cogito
the nonvisible
to death

It really freaks me out
the power yet
of the slipping word
madman's billboard

Ten Commandments still capped in text

There are "no unnecessary burdens"—Think of my mother
having an MRI, rolled in, singing, to the tube. The technician:
"For some people this is impossible."

He cross-eyed looks on onions and buys potatoes.

5. You take me to lunch

With "balled fists"
Unit of meaning
The huge sphere
of influence into which I step
(already written for me, or writing
itself as I write it, ahead of my pen
in front of allegiance) short legs
identify the runner as a child by intervals

between muffled footfalls
You claim William Blake for your own

and then the child
snuck up behind me and stood there
I could feel the nothing displaced
by the child's waiting
on the back of my head.
"And what is the last name of your wife?"

Blake.

Even just the apprehension of it
all these things are hard to do at once
A trot between the eggs,
the customer demand

In God's dictionary
the words "faithful," "humble,"

and "famous"
are synonymous. Right on

with the new facility.

Just the erotic life, please
your erotic life together "a whole other language":
the word *violator* is hidden somewhere in *parvenu*

6. Howler

These people tend to act differently
A smaller group, but they tend to act better

For I am the genie of self-critique

increased sensitivity to one color
next to another: the bluejay's
head being slightly empurpled
beside the royal blue
of his tailfeathers, psychic
school of emboldenment.
Develop this further 'til

Can you be more specific?

I might like
music more if I knew that you liked it.
I have made the world ready for me.

Never-entered

Criminal Justice System

I discover I have nothing to hide
Now stand up and face me.
And then I felt queasy
              in the balance.
And then I gave in to the next part.
My family . . . *mi familia*
For some reason
              I am honest

I'm in trouble, Dad, it's my recombinant [ ]
I'm in trouble, Officer, it's my degenerate [ ]

I'm in trou . . . tru . . . truck.
I have a baby.
I write in English within the confines
              and that's a big conflict

I advise you now to stand up and face me
within the structure

Mama didn't raise no fools

He died before we could honor
him correctly. Candied

impulse through the brain.
Your will subverted

that's a tree, a treatment,
a genealogy. Oddly enough if I need something

someone is sure to give it to me.
To supply me with it. Oddly enough,

it's not about cutting slack
but about positive reinforcement

Detergent in the sense that it is

emergent

deterrent
where the nascent

meets the latent
I put my tongue in the path

dug up some chestnuts.
"We'll keep looking

for a place for you
inside of nature"

I can't remember how I died.
Writing something down at the same time

the grave had been disturbed.
Next thing you know, I'm making

an entry in my diary: No use
letting it get cold.

Don't look in the basket

but to wind up
loving its permanence,
waking up to contents

I get glimpses, typically.

The things you tell your unborn
children: "You'll be many
different masters, but all the same
slave."

A phalanx of puppetry,
p's in ascension: preeminent,
prime minister. Excuse me:
Why do you sit forward like that?

Oh that's easy (direct confrontation), because
I have this cumbersome weight on my back. God
is in the desperation
in fallopian tube

in porn
in coffee can
in arsenal

there must be something extraordinary going on in my face.
A long and rambling conversation.

En Plein Air

The winter sun calls us
to sit down under a tree on the hard
plaza near the shoeshiner.

degraded
after the Reconstruction
tucked your tail under

And when the French say
"le racisme" they refer to
a distraction. The French
they are in reverse and referential
as a consequence

a nostalgia directly related
to the quality of light; this is quality
light.

Hey,
and it's not a location anymore, it's

where the logic falls apart
this is why it is so subversive for those
Chinese girls to wear those
big clunky shoes

Dana Plato Fatality

Hungry for strangers
it's that time of the month

Making funny faces in the mirror—
　　　　　take it one step further and
make funny shapes with your body

Pose as Shiva with your palms out toward the mirror

Suffused with that irritant
Parroted internationally

known as train wreck

With oncoming blindness
With incoming invisible

Hungry for appetite
it's that kind of collapsed conveyance

fantasia of recall
unchecked by the poke of vestigial freckles

it's unfortunately visible

and she's crying in the mirror like a pornstar

Neurological

Horrifying emotional
insignificant chin
with irrepressible disdain
regard said construct
said "wobbly chicken neck"
and the unforgivable ways I've felt
in my life

No one pays me for it
Trains today roll
collating the above
I'm not feasting on affect
Immemorial.
Now I'll never find out what happened
to that corpse in the
crennelated
never-entered

Farm Stand

Struck by your bohemian demeanor

Event no reason
to come in like a lamb
or
rest immovably folded, a sick pigeon in a foyer

• • •

I am teaching him the proportions
What a tired relationship.

Profit margin to cost of production

When first you get your hands on me

A different consortium

Diffident
Sibilant
They fly to the region
of your concentration

• • •

That's not a door that's a window
it's all just semantics (tired
phrase), the package we are offering in proportion
to the publisher's demands

the dimensions of your principles
parallel to the alignment of my relativism

the lengths we go to to expatriate ourselves

• • •

Holding hands with a lower life-form,

friendly.

Within the Greek-American community

smiles all around for everybody

without event,

without moment

• • •

It's a *mitzvah*

lack of self-consciousness
now I've learned the word

the holes in my lobe
will never heal

peripheral appeal
I will buy the young man breakfast
without asking him to adhere

Promise me not to waste his sweet young life

. . .

Struck by your bohemian demeanor

we are engaged to move upland to the site of your endeavor

Where your accented speech, your general good cheer,
is the norm and not the crater.

. . .

Come in   friendly
forcing fluids
through the alien filter

Things of Beauty from the Story:

I wish we had a microwave but we don't

Suburban friends
in full flower
raw-boned
the heart-warming way

House Party

1. LE WEEKEND

Holden Caulfield, of noble birth
can't stand the flits.
With my shapely ankles
I protest, indentured
like the rest. "I wasn't
supposed to live this long"—

The kind of open face
perfect for pictures
outgrown its humanity
"Peerage not all it's cracked up to be—"
that's self-made Cyril Connolly on

any one of a dozen aristocracies.
The trees know I am too tenderhearted
for clearing the slated.
A sluggish yellow jacket on its back
stings once you help it right itself.
Like a weekend in Southampton.

2. THE BIG SNOW

Out of nothing
how do you conceive of anything?

By imagining what the better part
might applaud.

Lucidity, the group of you together
untold days under a blanket
of storm warning: You had *better not*
better not
better not
go outside:
any minute the curtain may fall.

. . .

You have been trying to say something amusing
for the better part
of a quarter . . . the party
is losing patience. It means something,
that is clear, but without charm
is it worth simply meaning? Oxygen

is stolen from the furnace by the fire;
really it is the fire*place* that is to blame,
she's a great whore.
She demands,

and we sit by her side for hours
at a time, implying nonnarrative
by our rapt attention. The gilded

edge of chicanery
on which guests leap and sputter
not in mockery but in
assumed identity: *We will warm you! If not*

we will chase you out of your home
and into a night far blacker than any
from which you have recused us.

Have no fear. The Big Snow
will never find us.
It mistrusts us, essentially.

3. PASTORAL EPITHALAMION

Given ideal circumstances,
in an ideal world,
the actress and the intellectual
will lie down together
and she will learn vocabulary
words; her "views" will inflame
him in his ironic distance. Around
the table in the candlelight bugs
keep off and we are talking
about the right thing—capital
punishment—for more than the slotted
two and a quarter hours. No
conclusion can be final
when we are all together
in it. When can I join
your wealthy congregation?
Where is the evangelist
when his service is required?

And where are my people?
The telltale mistresses
by which ye shall come to know me
by the authority vested in me.
Entertain a new thought—our Polish
beauty, promised to a young doctor
has married instead his brother the mensch;
her strong jaw and weak eyes
afford a cross-breeze

on the daybed in the back den,
resting away from the party
for three and a quarter hours.
If she only knew how much we disparage her.

4. Bob's Your Buddha: Dine Out on This

"I always loved how he was with people,
Bob the Farmer. 'Bring it ON,'* he'd say,
rotund—be it early dementia, exploitation,
chronic asthma, fatal allergic
reaction to peanuts lying dead on the road
while the other bike racers sped
past. 'Bring it on!'* Pale dawn

rising over the rich fields, immense,

intense, cosmic plenty

they grow on stalks

Brussels sprouts, and in the late fall
almost frozen, really, you get down
on the hard ground and cut the little
spheres away.

A militant stance against encroaching
cynicism, the tilling and seeding of wintering
crops such as rye, such as oats.

'It's he-eere,'† he might say, regarding
early darkness, death or dearth, waist-high
flooding, snotty kid, corroded

fruit, the fatal flaw, the stink of rot, a friend's
betrayal, abstract thinking

about kharma, on the subject of meaninglessness."

†*It's here* refers to nothing
Bring it on is invitation

5. Everyone's Mobilized: A Ghost Story

"Everyone's invited! 'If your whirlpool
has ceased to pull its weight,
it is enough to enter the Grand Park
and reclaim a louche point
on its perimeter. You know
it is circular and there is no corner,
hence this cannot be a story
of redemption or deep failure.'
A bloodletting, by any
stretch of the imagination.

The brunt—the thrust—as though a character,
three-dimensional as a caramel
reclaimed a mobile horse off of a left-
over carousel.

Indulge the horse: nostrils flared above a mouth that
sneers without rancor, only with fervor and the pulling bit.
Above it all we have rolling eyes, stationary intent,
inside on the outside, something
finally fully present in the moment,
however wooden, however painted."

6. SUNDAY MORNING; OR, INSTEAD OF SERVICES

How can I tell you that we are at a poetry reading?
At the mercy of potentially cruel masters.
In this case, I won't take no for an answer.
Vexed the glassy surface of Gene Kelly.

To be a laborer! Psychoanalysis?
Or to labor in reviewing
it fell off the back of a truck
and I picked it up.

Cyril Colony? A pastry chef
a barber's shop
". . . for my troubles
I am invited everywhere—once.

And oh, the pain of feeling
I would never belong to the despised . . ."[1]

poetry reading. Not apprehension
but collection. No time for philosophizing:
the space between the shapes in its proper
place, my ass

and the hard
folding chair,

my ass and the poets of my generation
and the poets of your generation,

thinking practically the idea,
we none of us can believe

the same simple truths, the gems.

[1] Ben Sonnenberg, *Lost Property: Memoirs and Confessions of a Bad Boy*, Counterpoint Press, 1999.

7. BELL RINGER FOR WEATHER

Cold starts with the sun gone down
warming up at early dawn

Overcast at break of day
clearing up intermittently

Thrice-demented clouds of
country occlusion—*where have our
ambitions gone?*

We will wait for the sun to get high
and hit the house.

*Penetrate the house, ambient
tenor*

Perpetrate the house, an insurrection
of joists

No adolescent fervor but a
languor, progressive
no longer.

• • •

All day it never warms
up like it ought. *Triple
negative.* The severe

face of summer passing over
our heads, big Gentile face. Parade

around, early fall, mock you
the chill of excised
exposure. Each fattened cell foregrounded

by the light of recumbent November's
April. Our heads

caught in the lamplight
of weather passing over

caught splayed upon the pillow, mouths
in incandescent chorus

caught napping.

As if overheard

After Balthus

Norman Rockwell is my favorite painter.

It closely resembles the face I wore
before I was born.

Sybil

1. These are the vague demands you make on me

2. (that I) assemble
   (to) recollect
   (to) decode
   ( ) associate

3. that I admit, fraught with difficulty, reintegration
   is no day at the beach in eggshell tints
   "The inmates start to get brave and a little crazy"
   when they hear that friendly voice—the matron.

4. (But that's also my mind, lost)
   Her epic poem on the constraints society places on the

5. misunderstood.

6. Everything can't be . . . a product of imagination
   The reasons for doing this are many *and* variable
   and *I'm ready for my close-up* . . .

7. You know that scrimshaw's been outlawed
   Finally, they tried an antipsychotic on me
   This had an unexpectedly positive effect
   on the general population, the dissimulation,
   the oppression

8. the faint aroma of performing seals.
   With that same arrogant look on his face,
   a man related to you commits suicide
   in a dark room, tonight. I am "a psychic,"
   but she is psychic
   Sarcasm not in her repertoire.

9. If you are transparent it is for transcendence.
   A good friend, she hears herself telling me
   "there is more to my essential character,
   more that is most essentially me."

10. Don't think of how much time we've wasted
    blood on your protruding lower lip
    the dead hours are really dead
    (inchoate)
    (insensate)

11. with such good will and sex
    appeal young girls descend
    the staircase. My ears ring
    and my vision fails. I must be
    speaking the truth

12. . . . the cat came back,
    padding on sore paws over ninety miles
    to the old homestead,
    destroyed by fire

13. the bull moose lets out a roar.
    Making the music I'm famous for.
    Rope's indulgence gives

14. . . . the void rushes in.
    Is that a musket mounted
    on the wide-planked wall?
    Or a yoke?

15. Something brainless about that half
    of the bracket.
    The registration
    of sound on my mind,

16. it was as though she'd placed them there for me to see.
    I am only in the picture at one end
    —this is probably more than you ever wanted to know
    about me. Men outside.
    I'm a woman
    in a pastel field.
    What I want out of a

    fuck-scene: continuity. In
    fear of you.

Roman Polanski

Straining under you
I don't have the right kind of mind.
Or maybe I'm just not trying hard enough
on a certain level

it disintegrates into random locution
I heard a description of an execution
the bed a rumpled mess,
the sky above roseate with storm clouds,

a Rubaiyat kingdom of cloud.
Sleeping with you is like sleeping outdoors,
a thin skin or shell of firmament presiding.
I'll only go with a man

on a certain level.
Now we are behind the road,
following the long, alternative
power lines. I mean to alert you to the
great holes in the sky. My sunglasses, which correspond
to the dodging sun.

I'm watching the way the mind and the body go
together. There are those who kill others and eat them,
but I do not relate this to any specific incident.
The spicy taste of nasturtium, which is not quite a flavor.

We lay like a log,
(his penis)
a hot-water bottle,

a hose, a reminder.
An armful, a palliative, one gorgeous
kiss at the terminal.
You have to pay attention to the order

*"If you ain't lovin
then you ain't livin"*
riding this fine line between the absurd

and the fantastical. Just yesterday
he said to me "I don't need to tell you
what we make with each other
here." Because I spoke

through my skin he was fully
realized. At the flower's center a burst,
a passionate expression. An expression
of passion. We long for (among

other things)
you to understand.
*"My wife is dead . . . absolutely
mad, I said."*

The articulation of her limbs—lithe, tawny
as two stewardesses, workmanlike
as a metaphor, bespeaking
I fucked him when he had a fever. Purely

experiential. His skin was tight and dry, there was no
lubrication: He burned everything up. His eyeballs
were glassy: The inside of his mouth smelled like blood.
Imagine that there

is a mountain range, that cloudbank hanging out
over the cemetery. He never thanked me

for my wordless communication. When I
stroked his big head. Pressing
essence from infirmity.
"What did that feel like?"

(after) it's all over. "I dunno.
Warm." Come over here and
fuck me with that
long thing *So far he has yet to*

Good enough for folk music

The song goes on longer than we expect
because it is from another culture: collected,
as it were. Folks (people)
with meaning or without, a gentle
ponytail hanging down the middle of his back.
And when you say *culpable*
it makes me want to kiss you
smack on the vocabulary

and that is condescension.
We have seen the man perform in his hometown
(I am increasingly right. You must apologize)

and the yokels talked me into staying late.
It was a good room. It was a good house
the crowd warmly appreciative
not to go so far as a square dance.
Unguent created

unctuous role model

play gets feverish
in a flurry of miscegenation. Folks, people, settle down,
we're not doing brain surgery here after all.

Broken Sound Parkway

Rising in the east
a pale broadcast

my face will burn

my face will not burn owing
to the unguent

of childlike demeanor

• • •

Reading only exegesis, one might
wrongly assume
a posture of contemplation.
Not earned but bargained for.
"Hi, I'm Mr. Survival!"
The advantage of narrative:

East River through
a moving window, the car's moving
window. I wish to emphasize the East River.
I love my body,
and have returned to it.

• • •

Anybody:
Projection on weather

novelistic machine
Summer dying
heavy on the vine
Winter attendant
avuncular pederast

Characters coming in
off the streets and home to roost,
red-breasted
red-blooded:

Demented, spectral
little-black-girl asleep
in a chair in the dim room,
daylight failing, neck
uncharacteristically bent.

You've nursed her back to health
and now you're close as close can be

book without integrity,
with built-in obsolescence

face relaxed into an expression
of dismal contemplation

impression of rain-soaked
lovely to glance at but

inappropriate therefore for posterity.

. . .

And so now I know the meaning of *bloodcurdling*;
an Opening in the Park,
space-time continuum a crumpled
rising shrouded heap, vitally
singular tragedy. "What
an incredible face," she tried to say,
just for show.

How does that go? *You know*
one, you take one—
You take what you see.

At the expense of my own face, there are images
I can use, and images I can't. Leaving me
without gender, without preference

and all the genius flying out the window.
That's the last time I do anything
wordless.

. . .

I am released once more into the night.
It is cold, literally, and literally
quite dark. I make it harder than it has to be.
The perfume of longing for elsewhere.

The interrogative

Soulless evening.
And then I was assaulted by
the morning smells of tearless
smoke, street food on fire. Also a punctured
odor of mirror.

Down to earth, yet hobbled
by an inheritance.

Evaluation Day,
and then I went on to do some
soul-searching. Crass and dry, but

begun in a spirit of optimism
to take everything down in the dawn
to be a leader in one's field.

Hot morning of the revolution
empathy extended even beyond
the sick orange cats
at the Chinese grocer. Even unto her

Yellow skin of the cow
The minute the cold air hit my eyes I was
seized. If everything seems forced it may be due
to a preemptive

pale and frozen maiden
weeping as she walks
not carrying the loss well

interrogative. Oh, and it's a windy one,
a pleasantry, internal logic
rescuing each gust from each prospective
barrier. All university
is not the same university. And

people don't always do what they say
they want to do. Her
face fell.

The Wreck of the SS *Supernatural*

Sweet night air
it's the little things. The animalism
of your contract, your
fiendish protraction.

First chipmunk, then frog, then
finally bird dying in the room between
our vehicles. Things full of sugar
and substance. Prevarication:

there is a time
there was a time
there was a place,
(we all have access)

where one thing follows
another and the flowering shrubs,
the high tall grasses,
the swamps and marshes

fill the air with their
white negotiation,
wanton in the dark when
they do this. In the dark

is where you'll find it.
Then I met the shell and the shell

was real, every vatic pronouncement
prevaricated: The mother

dies, after all. Should I be afraid
of your long memory? The little
bark-boring beetle, without any English name.
Briar, no exodus:

Stay where you are
I beg of you. Shack in the field. Origin
misled and the grandiose
unnamed of nascent

blue—generality made specific
by its emptiness.
There were a few things available to us
that were perfect just the way we found them. This is a specific

reference and not abstract: grandiose generality made specific . . .
And as often happens, the faint taste
of something good to eat
comes into my mouth

from an unknown source. You could say
mysterious. You could say *origin*. In the turgid urban
locale. And I grow power hungry,
as Demi Moore does in *Disclosure*.

Another brainless preadolescent says "My ass is for sale"

for Calvin Klein

Oh toddler, with so much dull gleam in your gaze
my pant leg is of indeterminate hem: It is neither high
nor full, rich nor strong. But it is lyric in intent

—not interested in doing any smothering right now,
thanks. Beware of zealots: It upsets me to learn,
for instance,

that my mother is a whore
and that you fucked her all night long.
Sucking in gobbets of coldest air
a root-ball growing into chain-link

—the comparison is inevitable: newly humorless
mature syntax
shorn of affect.
With seed in hand, can sowing be far off?

. . .

Little pitchers
go into business
for themselves

the gorge rises

and is subsumed
party favor
why let that sexy body go to waste in a carrel?

you are far more picturesque than I could ever hope to be

dressed perfectly for the weather for once
What does it afford me
with regards to an unbroken celebrity?

. . .

Your name in lights
sensitive subject.

Early spring. As manifested in the clearance *brack*
of February. This is the season that will come to be called
"my" season, if I understand you correctly—

It's like what you read about: I'd never been
pleasured by a building
before; the afterimage of Bilbao's curvilinear
edifice rising like a sundae between spread
legs rings forever in my mind like a popular song

grounded in social reality
but with a presumption of cerebral over
political activity

Considerable Expense

at The Drawing Center, 2001

Which charm?
Oh, I thought you said . . .
A miraculous accusation,
All capitalized
indictment: Nothing Purple
Comes Near

the Face.

How to create a language
in relation to truth. *It's a very special thing
what did you make of it?* It is

an ethics of representation:

the difference between having something shoddy to say
and not having anything to say—My Wrist Slit!
and the blood that emerges is a valley
of blood, a vale of blood

stanzas and stanzas wrought or writ
in blood. "Objectification is the structure"

(of the table, of the rose). The stink of the mid-eighties

is on you and there is nothing you can do.

. . .

Insert a mordant social utility
evading stylistic conformity (social realism) really—
in favor of emotional realism?
And that's not solipsistic.

Poured it down the funnel.

. . .

I had the value-free feeling tonight
that nothing was as good
as it should be—prompted.

A triad of disciples, all grand
and living up to it
but really after all
wiped out in the shade
of reputation.
Perhaps the room is sucking talent

Perhaps the walls are greased with signage
with pleasure engorged the mixture

of the personal and the professional

Perhaps we've entered a domain
of hyper-Schadenfreude
where perceptual vertiginism
can be observed

trying for that eighties art school look.
A glamour kiss, by which we all are elevated.
The dynamic principle of the extremities of vitality.

I'm trying to make sense!
and it is barely keeping me alive.
For once you mustn't snicker.

Sunshine

for Ralph Fiennes

Does anybody know whose white dog it is
terrifying up by the graveyard? Methodist,
it made me turn around and walk

the other way—I could not get by it on foot.
It galloped toward me

the boring stank of ambivalence

"discontinued"
White curtains
aesthetic appreciation

You are the sunshine
Several songs
recommence

to reference; you pointed out long ago
a sort of patchwork quality
and I said *Turn away your malodorous gaze*

you shite Scottish bastard
never to place a comma again.

Corn for food or
corn for feed
or seed corn; that's the story:

All my needs met on 11th Street
all my needs met on the inside
In the little spot—the baby voice—

speaking voice of the singer
Intestate. I can't imagine what they have to say to each other
over there in the morning

first thing in the morning to each other in small voices
and doing a survey is logistically
prohibitive. *What a relief!*

Unless you're drawn and quartered
the joints stay in their sockets
blushing in conversation
with animal fame.

Invidious Comparison

Fat kids of the South
with early breasts
in the swimming pool outside

and as rites of passage go,
it's a benign and thoughtful entry.

There is an expression I keep hearing
I wanted to use it. I looked for it in popular music:
If she's a nun then I'm the pope.

Don't ask me what I'm doing.
I'm thinking *it's only this beautiful*
here. Now my body is made of long-standing
spirituality, by nature benign. Don't laugh: I'm a

Lotus-flower Gentle Sitting-still Woman.

And another paradigm slips into
place like the diamond it
sounds like. I'm no go-getter—
what am I after all but a

raft.

As If by Magic, Context

You said you wanted to sit in a pool of light

there are some things about you that I don't like. *That,*
not *which.* In a rabbit warren

the broad avenue
begins embattled, the Coleridge figment,
or the dream with the scrambled things
in it always being prime.

Did you ever think that you didn't love?

and the reverse made impossible
demands. The walls inside

feel like they're on fire

with the one I love. During the night

the house cooled.

In Egypt the Traveler Falls into the Arms of a Despairing Stranger

Standing water, the full sentence
Canister, line of thought
industrial seedpod, the
Bootblack, the impermeable

trace, a child's pathos forked over—
How long have I known you?

An element, too hot to stay sitting here
Forever in the midday inadvisable
The concerted, the concertina
The friendship the unaccounted for
The piquancy of *get back, come back to my hovel*
where I fear I am the only inhabitant
And that I would write a novel
out of the irony, the canvassed madrigal.
There's a whole-cloth permeability to these facts I must relate.

How long have we known each other? Now
I must rephrase the understanding:
"Though you admire me always from afar
Yet I still repay the debt." The art
is standing under
aspect consortium,
the sign of dignitaries—"My word!"

mannerism no more superficial
than a daylily. Cut down the torch it's burning.

Lamb, Willow: An Arch Dolefulness
Has Taken Me This Far

If you like Chance
and you think you might live forever
listen: They say death comes to us all.
They say: Tuesday Death comes to everybody.

Then if you really think about it,
it starts to seem unlikely,

dust the most forgiving
of all elements. Rinsed clean, I am, I say, through
no particular effort.

Once more I am in the right place but with the wrong feelings.
Festival of Mysteries, Carnival of Absolute Purchasing Power.

Damp-earth smell rises up
from the rigid enclosure,
terraced zone of eternal rest. I brought myself here
for one whole day; I bought an all-day
pass. Flashbulb pops off in the exclusive crypt:

You said you wanted to see . . .

Here is a machine that kills
cancer. By liquefying
cells and freezing them and then cracking the bad cells
into a million pieces and vacuuming them up with a tiny

nozzle. It's so effective, we are all
living long lives. You made your living

as a nurse in the old country.
Only the knowledge that I had done it before

allowed me to think that I could possibly
do it again. The demystification of meantime
into a magic circle—it is, essentially,
mine: my job to make it smarter, a dog
and puppy show. Illimitless

deep pathos of the infant cosmology;
amusement park of abbreviation.
More important the unlimited freefall
in the spot you bury your demon:

It goes down,
while you grow up, and last the centuries
as a lamb or willow

Lamb or willow,
wherever you go,

fear
the living *and* the dead
inertial and nocturnal
energies a winding shroud

(I was born
with a yellow brain
and cannot make up stories)

it can be as short as you want it
it can be as long as you want it.
That's not your temperature, that's
a homemade contaminant.

Spacious Sity of Eternal Rest
of rectangular shape wherein I will find

coagulate.

Rinsed clean, I am, I say, and
it hardly matters

Spring, Summer, Winter

From the land, the water
from the water, the land

instrument to medium in the meantime

stuck out here in the devastation in the forest
in the middle of fucking nowhere
between landmass and incontinence

camp and derangement, the more songlike
the further we row
from our figmented shore